GOD'S RAINBOWS ARE FOREVER

Ann Wilson

Illustrated by Pam Day

WestBow Press books may be ordered through booksellers or by contacting:

WestBow Press
A Division of Thomas Nelson & Zondervan
1663 Liberty Drive
Bloomington, IN 47403
www.westbowpress.com
844-714-3454

Interior Image Credit: Pam Day

Scripture quotations marked KJV are taken from the King James Version.

ISBN: 978-1-6642-8714-3 (sc)
ISBN: 978-1-6642-8715-0 (e)

Library of Congress Control Number: 2022923321

Print information available on the last page.

WestBow Press rev. date: 04/26/2023

WESTBOW
PRESS®
A DIVISION OF THOMAS NELSON
& ZONDERVAN

I am dedicating this book to my grandma, Texie Hicks. Grandma was the most loving and caring person the Lord ever placed in our lives. She had the love of God in her and shared it with all! Grandma always welcomed everyone in for a meal or a snack no matter if they were family, friend, or stranger. Her home was the most welcoming place you could ever go. When you met her, you felt the Lord's goodness, love, and mercy! That's who Grandma was.

Introduction

"And the bow shall be in the cloud; and I will look upon it, that I may remember the everlasting covenant between God and every living creature of all flesh that is upon the earth" (Genesis 9:16, KJV).

"And God said unto Noah, This is the token of the covenant, which I have established between me and all flesh that is upon the earth" (Genesis 9:17, KJV).

On a beautiful spring morning, Zephora and her grandma were out on the porch, rocking in their rocking chairs. The sun was trying to shine through the clouds while it was still raining.

Zephora was singing, "Rain, rain, go away! Come again another day. Little Zephora wants to play!"

Then, all of a sudden, the rain stopped. The sun popped out, and a beautiful rainbow appeared. The rainbow stretched from one end of the sky all the way to the other.

Grandma was still rocking in her chair when she heard Zephora shout, "Come quick, Grandma; there are beautiful colors in the sky!"

Grandma jumped out of her chair and rushed to see what Zephora had spotted. She said, "How glorious and beautiful these colors are! This is a rainbow."

Zephora said, "Where did it come from? How did it get in the sky?"

Grandma answered, "It sounds like it's time for me to tell you the true story of the rainbow."

About that time Zephora's friend Eli came up on the porch. "Hi, Eli," said Grandma and Zephora.

Then Grandma said, "I'm so glad you came over. I was getting ready to tell the true story of the rainbow in the sky."

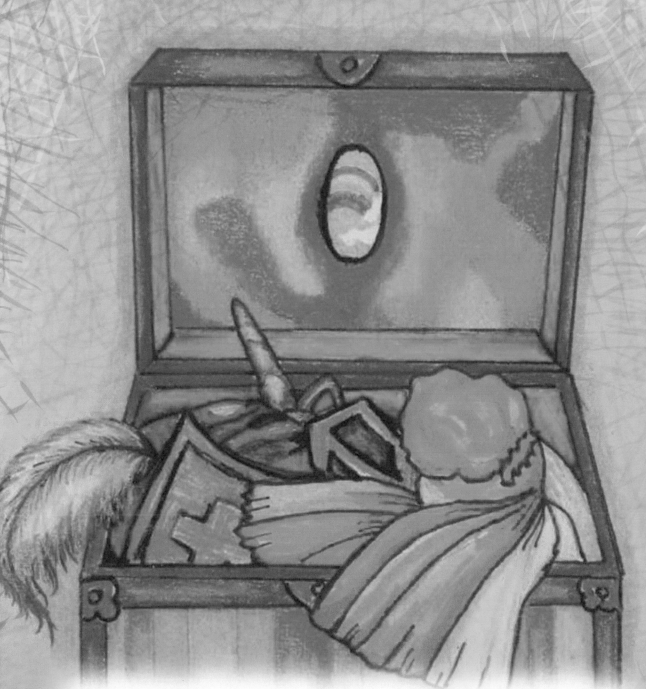

"I think it would be fun if you and Zephora acted out the story while I tell it. I have a trunk of old costumes inside."

Zephora and Eli both shouted with excitement.

"Oh yes, it will be fun!" said Zephora.

"Well, let's get you two dressed and get started on the story."

A long, long, time ago, the people on earth were not keeping the commandments of the Lord.

They were very wicked. They did a lot of mean things.

There was a man named Noah whom loved God; he was a very nice man. God told Noah He was going to destroy the people because they were so wicked.

God told Noah to build an ark for him, his family, the animals, and the birds to live in. God told Noah it would rain for forty days and forty nights. He told Noah that all the people, animals, and birds that did not go into the ark would die.

13

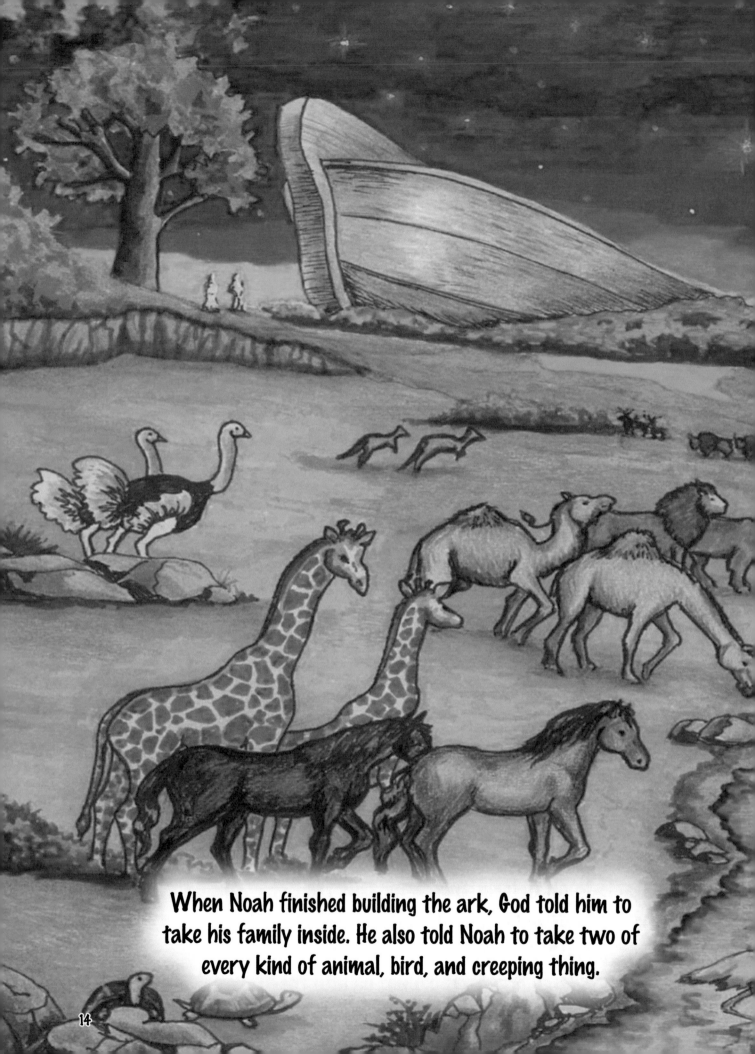

When Noah finished building the ark, God told him to take his family inside. He also told Noah to take two of every kind of animal, bird, and creeping thing.

Noah obeyed and took a male and female of each creature with him. Then God shut the door to the ark.

It rained forty days and forty nights. Noah and all the creatures were safe on the ark, while all the other people and creatures on earth died.

After the water dried up, God told Noah that he, his family, the animals, the birds, and the creeping things could leave the ark.

When they left the ark, Noah built an altar and offered burnt offerings unto the Lord.

The Lord made a covenant with Noah; a covenant is like a promise. He told Noah he would never again destroy the whole earth, the people, or the creatures with a flood.

Now every so often after it rains, you will see a beautiful rainbow. When you see the rainbow, you will remember the promise God made to Noah.

After Grandma finished telling the story, Zephora said, "I love the story of the rainbow! Can you tell it again?"

Printed in the United States
by Baker & Taylor Publisher Services